TOBY SCHMITZ is a leading Australian actor and award-winning playwright. His first play *dreamalittledreamalittle* was staged downstairs at Belvoir St Theatre (1998). Schmitz won the Sydney Theatre Company's Patrick White Playwrights' Award (2002) with his play *Lucky* and the Australian National Playwrights' Centre/ New Dramatists Award (2004) for *Chicks Will Dig You! Chicks* was performed as part of Company B's 2003 B Sharp season. His other plays include *This Blasted Earth* (written with Travis Cotton and Tim Minchin), *Pan, Cunt Pi, fifteen and then some* and *Grazing the Phosphorus*, commissioned by the National Institute of Dramatic Art. In 2007, he wrote and directed *Capture the Flag* for Tamarama Rock Surfers at The Old Fitzroy Theatre. It toured nationally for Playwriting Australia in 2011.

From left: Robin Goldsworthy as Albert, Anthony Gee as Karl and Sam North as Herret in the 2007 Tamarama Rock Surfers production at the Old Fitzroy Theatre in Sydney. (Photo: Cam Baird)

CAPTURE THE FLAG

TOBY SCHMITZ

CURRENCY PLAYS

First published in 2012
by Currency Press Pty Ltd,
PO Box 2287, Strawberry Hills, NSW, 2012, Australia
enquiries@currency.com.au
www.currency.com.au

Reprinted 2021

NATIONAL LIBRARY OF AUSTRALIA CIP DATA

Author:	Schmitz, Toby.
Title:	Capture the flag / Toby Schmitz.
ISBN:	9780868199375 (pbk.)
Series:	Current theatre series.
Subjects:	Youth and war—Germany—Drama.
	War—Drama.
Dewey Number:	A822.4

Capture the Flag was created with assistance from the Commonwealth Government through the Australia Council, its arts funding and advisory body.

Contents

Typeset by Dean Nottle for Currency Press.
Cover design by Katy Wall for Currency Press.
Cover image: Sam North as Herret, Robin Goldsworthy as Albert and Anthony Gee as Karl (Photo: Cameron Baird).

Currency Press acknowledges the Traditional Owners of the Country on which we live and work. We pay our respects to all Aboriginal and Torres Strait Islander Elders, past and present.

BACKGROUND

German children had been pointed towards rigorous physical activity before the Nazis. But after 1933 'action' became the spine of all Nazi policy concerning youth. The education system was Nazified and Hitler Youth (Hitler Jugend) membership became compulsory. By the time war started, nearly seven and a half million of Germany's nine million children were HJ members.

The goals of the youth movement were strength, bravery and devotion to Hitler above all else. Experience was praised, learning dismissed. Labour, pain and endurance were idealised as part of every child's duty, the honour being in the task. Language was militarised, phrases such as 'leadership principle' and 'the battle of work' were born. As the war ground on, physical activity became early basic training. Hiking trips and running races, by war's end, had been replaced with marching, spying and military manoeuvres.

Parents could and did restrict their children from Hitler Youth activities, but, especially in areas where leadership was efficient, life could become extremely dangerous for parents, teachers and children who resisted.

Hitler Youth were highly visible throughout the Third Reich, organising local events: 'Jew-baiting' in the street, singing and marching in ever-increasing parades, hollering outside the houses of children who resisted membership, collecting scrap metal, in charge of fire drills. German adults—be they powerless appeasers, 'ten percent Nazis' or fervent believers—had placed nearly every German child in military school, complete with uniforms. So, by the end, parents had to watch many of Germany's youngest sons charge into action, dying to be real soldiers, and zealous ones at that.

Like many, Hitler idealised youth. Nazism idealised everything to fit its ever-expanding brief: Germany, war, killing, dying, tragedy, art, history, women, race. For every image of the ideal that Nazism conjures—the breathtaking rallies, Speer's banners and spotlights, the brave and devoted soldier—we need only reflect on their counterpoints—the skeletal stacks of stiff corpses at the camps, Dresden cindered, or the pathetic crime-scene images of those who shot or poisoned themselves before they could be hanged—to leave us deep in human ponder as to how insane the gap between the ideal and the real world became. The notion that these people were products of their time does little to dispel the worrying fact that these people were indeed people, and they prospered not so very long ago.

The image that perhaps best represents both the fall and myth of National Socialism is the black-and-white film footage of a ruined Hitler, on his last birthday, pinning medals to Hitler Youth boys outside his bunker as the Russian troops crawl towards him, only suburbs away. None of the boys have known any leader but Hitler, and some are aged just twelve. By then the divisions between Hitler Youth, Volkssturm, Wermacht, SS and civilian had been dismissed by Hitler. Even girls were ordered to man anti-aircraft guns, a complete betrayal of his countless decrees and theories insisting German women could never engage in battle. The boys, although weary, beam proudly at meeting the Führer they have sworn their lives to. They are the last, if not the cream of the Hitler Youth. They had survived years of Allied bombing raids night and day, artillery barrage, fighting the bitter Russian troops and tanks with bicycles and single-shot rocket launchers, and now for many of them the fall of Berlin was a glorious opportunity to fulfill the myth they had been repeating from the beginning of their indoctrination. To spill their blut for the Führer. Their motto, like the SS, was simply 'Führer, command—and we will follow'.

By May 1945, the scattered groups of surviving children in each basement and shell hole faced stupefying circumstances, and sometimes choices, that betrayed their short lives. Many looked to their superiors only to find them either killing themselves, dead or disappeared. There were no men left. Children fought alongside pensioners.

Those who lived and fell under the Soviet occupation faced the dawn of a new war, and more immediately, starvation, exploitation, wholesale rape and murder. The occupying soldiers from Russia were brutal in exacting their revenge on Germans. Many of those who survived until the end of the occupation in 1989, especially women, only started telling their stories in their last years, such was the necessity, shame and tradition.

Most of the World War Two images I lingered over as a boy were those of Hitler Youth. My own fascist schooling, with its emphasis on sport, marching and violence, brought them into relief. The imagined dread of crunching tanks and furious men advancing on me, armed with only a small knife in an empty city, became the theme of my overactive nightmares. The boys boldly smiling in the photos seemed at once scary and innocent. Fierce. Then in the next shot: abject fear. The boys themselves embodied the twin image of myth and fall. In their faces.

I remember hearing the seminal story of HJ discipline at a young age, told to me, importantly, by my father. It was of a boy, driven by competitiveness and faith, reporting his parents to the Gestapo for selling ration tickets. Or for not attending a meeting, or telling the wrong joke. This idea that a boy could turn on the adults who forced him into premature adulthood always resonated.

Cases of children committing violence, murder, even war crimes in the name of nationalism emerge every day in the steppes of Russia, the villages of Africa, in Middle Eastern cities, the trailer parks of the United States, and the beach suburbs of Australia. A child, as J.M. Barrie pointed out, can be the cruelest thing in the world. Hitler was entirely correct when he saw the prepubescent boy as not only the future, but as a thing of unlimited potential. The points of light must never go out in our surveillance of what children believe. How determined can they be? How blind? How fast can they turn?

Toby Schmitz
March 2012

'Our flag is more to us than death.'
'Our Flag Is Guiding Us'
Hitler Youth anthem

Capture the Flag was first produced by Tamarama Rock Surfers at The Old Fitzroy Theatre, Sydney, on 9 May 2007 with the following cast:

KARL	Anthony Gee
ALBERT	Robin Goldsworthy
HERRET	Sam North
MATHILDE	Ella Scott Lynch

Director, Toby Schmitz
Set Designer, Leland Kean
Costume Designer, Lisa Walpole
Sound Designer, Jeremy Silver
Lighting Designer, Luiz Pampolha

CHARACTERS

KARL, 12

ALBERT, 12

HERRET, 8

MATHILDE, 15

NOTES ON SOUND

All sound from above—the rifles, troop trucks and the announcement—through a subterranean filter, as if through soil and concrete.

The original production used a soundscape at the beginning of the show that included the last thuds of artillery, the crunching sounds of occupation, gunfire, music, then just the sounds of the drains. Such a soundscape could shake the foundations.

For full effect, the grenade sequence may need to be stylised. Including ringing in the ears.

Music: Erik Satie—'Six Gnossiennes': No. 1: 'Lent'.

Three boys crouch ankle-deep in water in a narrow, deep, subterranean drainpipe. Darkness to the left and right.

A pipe above them leads up via metal rungs.

An oil lantern is slowly dying, leaving the extremities in pitch black.

KARL *and* ALBERT *are both twelve years old, but the actors needn't be.*

KARL's *Hitlerjungend uniform (black shorts, tunic, cap) is filthy and blood-caked and, though the scabbard is empty, complete. With no overcoat he is open to the elements. He has a serious injury he keeps to himself well.*

ALBERT's *uniform is piecemeal—some Hitlerjungend articles, some Jungvolk and some Wermacht, an official Hitlerjungend dagger on his hip. An adult infantry greatcoat, which hangs in the water.*

HERRET *is younger, the only child from a family of secret passive resisters. He wears a ceremonial Pimpf dagger over several layers of his own civilian clothes.*

It is extremely cold.

Above them, muffled, are the very occasional taps of rifle fire. These eventually stop.

Silences are beats and can be as long or short as necessary. They often whisper.

Silence.

HERRET: The light's going out.

ALBERT: Now Pimpfy has a voice. Shut up, Pimpfy.

    Silence.

HERRET: [*to himself*] We're inside a hedgehog.

    ALBERT *giggles.*

ALBERT: What? Did you hear that?

    Silence.

Tend the lamp. Our superior is thinking.

Silence.

KARL: So.

ALBERT: That's all you say. Let's go up. For a look at least.

HERRET: A huge hedgehog with spines pointing out.

ALBERT: My feet are—what? Speak like a defective again, go on, you're disturbing me now that you suddenly talk—talk sensible, runty, or not at all.

HERRET *stares at the lamp.*

Silence.

It's getting colder again. Not complaining.

Silence.

KARL: So.

ALBERT: So what?

KARL: That's the noise I make when I'm thinking, Wurtz, shut up.

Silence.

ALBERT: So. How are we going to bury so many people/ huh?

KARL *is overwhelmed by pains in his foot for a brief moment.*

KARL: Ugh.

ALBERT: It's always our job, and there's no room left. Dig through the last lot I guess.

KARL: Damn. These cramps.

HERRET: Me too, Mutti, in both legs.

ALBERT: Did you say Mutti?

HERRET: No sir, I said.

ALBERT *snorts.*

KARL *puffs quietly through pursed lips for a moment.*

ALBERT: Harden up. Nothing gets past the German soldier.

Silence.

So.

KARL: You have something to say say it.

ALBERT: You've had your five minutes. Orders, Jungzugfuhrer?

KARL: Smash ya jaw into your brain, shut up. Staying here till night, might organise a bit more off that horse.

ALBERT: How do you know it isn't night now?

Silence.

You were ordered to hold the position, are you ready to admit that?

KARL: Technically we all were.

ALBERT: Death or victory.

KARL: Orders. May have flown to the wind. So.

ALBERT: [*good-natured*] Technically you fucking failed.

KARL: To the last bullet, that was the order. I remember us running out of bullets.

ALBERT: Let me go up./ Hey.

KARL: Shh. Not happening.

ALBERT: For a look.

HERRET: It's dark, let's run to our homes—they're going to come down here.

KARL: Yes. We don't even know what you are. What are you?

Silence.

Tell me.

HERRET: The foundation of victory.

KARL: No I mean what's your unit?

HERRET: I haven't one.

ALBERT: Yes you do—he's bomb-blasted this one—you're defective.

HERRET: I'm not. I only got my dagger three weeks ago.

KARL: You haven't even passed your courage test?

HERRET *shakes his head.*

ALBERT: What?

HERRET: Don't make me do it.

KARL: Ha. I think you pretty much done it, kid.

HERRET: When can I go home?

ALBERT *turns on* HERRET, *furious.*

KARL: We need one to come down, Milk Cow, so we can recover its weapons. If we're to have any chance. Better to sweat it than bleed it.

HERRET: How can I sweat?

KARL: Put your hands under your arms like this.

ALBERT: [*to* HERRET] Where have you been? Answer me? Sitting at home sewing and pissing nursery rhymes in the fire? There's— By

the flag, you should be strung up. Where were you for the Year of
Trial, Year of Effort, Service— What's your excuse, traitor?

> ALBERT *has raised his voice.* HERRET *firms up.*

HERRET: I'm doing my part now, looking after my Mutti. Who's only
getting sicker—

ALBERT: You ignored your duty, so help you. You saw the deserters
swinging from the lampposts, didn't you?

KARL: He's done his duty.

ALBERT: He didn't do a thing. Don't look at me, look at the ground. What
a waste. You should be strung up really.

KARL: We aren't going to string you up, can you just be quiet?

> *Silence.*

ALBERT: Fidget said he saw Meyer strung up.

> *Silence.*

KARL: Impossible, he's a hero.

> *Silence.*

ALBERT: Where have the Red Cross gone, haven't seen them for days.
Cowards.

> *Silence.*

Where's he, do you think— Have they got to where he is yet? Jungzugfuhrer? Command, and we will follow. [*He laughs, once.*] They
were fuckin' big, weren't they Milk Cow?

> *Silence.*

They're bigger than I thought, I'll admit. Bigger than those ones they
had repairing the station, that's for sure. Bigger than you thought I
reckon, Jungzugfuhrer.

KARL: We've been over the size. The kid's pissing himself.

ALBERT: He's been pissing his pants since we found him.

HERRET: Haven't, promise.

KARL: It keeps you warm, good lad—/ survive.

ALBERT: I was repeating for a reason, we call it drill—I'm not scared—
we have new information we should drill it, review it, review it: The
enemy is really big. You could smell 'em too, huh. Like they said,

all the— But now we know exactly: Ivan smells like shit. I admit I was pissing it, top-shelf weed my pants at one point, I was—ha: They Were Big. But they couldn't get through that door, hey Milky, you were there for that, only reason we got through that hole… was 'cause he was that big. A goddamned fucking bear. So many of them too, huh? A, a, a pack a shitty bears.

Silence.

HERRET: Jungzugfuhrer? Do you think? My Mutti will be safe by now? She's over in/ Berliner Strasse—

ALBERT: We don't care where your fucking Mutti is. He doesn't care.

Silence.

Hey, which way did we come in again?

KARL *slowly puts his finger to his lips.*

Sir, permission to ask a question.

KARL: We're not talking.

ALBERT: Just point, I forget.

HERRET: Jungzugfuhrer?

KARL: [*with magnitude*] Please shut up.

ALBERT: Ah come on, we been down here too long, too long. Three days?

KARL: How do you know?

ALBERT: Whatever we're doing is wrong.

KARL: Who says? Scholl? My bicycle went through Scholly's throat, that's him on your collar, fool. Klober? Shit. The whole suburb's dec-imated, Ivan's main garrison advanced this morning, that's what all that rumble was, *but they'll be coming back,* to mop up, so.

ALBERT: So what? We'll be ready for all of them? It's time, time to move, admit. Admit: we should see what's down there.

HERRET: I don't want to, I/ just—

ALBERT: We don't care what you want, arsehole, some of our boys could need help or something, you wouldn't know.

KARL: [*looking*] That way's no good.

ALBERT: Don't pretend you know what's down there.

KARL: This is insubordination. Conserve your energies.

ALBERT: Why?

KARL: I have a feeling.

Silence.

ALBERT: Feelings are the/ enemies of...

KARL: / Enemies of decisions I know, I mean it's a gut feeling, like I won my dagger for in Hunting and Tracking: so sit on that.

ALBERT: Cheat.

KARL: Say that one more time.

Silence.

ALBERT: Ohh, that dagger you lost falling out the window, that one?

HERRET: Shh.

ALBERT: Back at the, um, what is it, capitulation? Don't you ever shoosh me.

KARL: It was a retreat.

ALBERT: The dagger out the window, that one, Karl?

KARL: You're wearing Fidget's knife, aren't you? Exactly, so, anyway so—so—so that's that, shut up. We regrouped and then we regrouped again, and now there's us, so.

ALBERT: Shh.

The distant rumble of vehicles above.

KARL: New.

ALBERT: New tanks.

KARL: Uh-uh, different sound completely.

They listen. KARL *tilts his head strangely.*

Troop carriers. Hear the difference?

ALBERT: [*flaring*] So what?

KARL: So we're not goin' up is what.

HERRET: Shh.

ALBERT: Not now, course not, we had all day.

KARL: I order you to shut up. They don't... they don't sound American, do they?

They get louder, then pass.

ALBERT: [*suppressing*] If Scholl and everyone else is decimashed, or whatever you called it, then you and your troop carrier, and your rank, can fairly get flogged: you're not even obeying orders!

KARL: I thought I was giving orders.

ALBERT: How do you even know what the American Jew gangsters sound like?

KARL: I know what the Ivan Jews sound like, we been listening all week!

ALBERT: Exactly! There are better, you know, hiding spots than a freezing sewer, that's all. Cheat.

KARL grabs ALBERT's head and squeezes.

KARL: I'll rip your lungs out. I won't think about it, I'll do it.

The last of the trucks vibrate down. It takes some time...

There are scouts down here, we must be twice as silent as them to ambush with any hope. At all. I won't say it again.

Silence.

HERRET: Please can I go?

ALBERT: Too bad. Your body belongs to your nation, kid. Rule One. You should know that. You should fucking know that.

HERRET: I know the ten rules.

KARL: The last bullet may be us, lads. Think about that and hold your rank.

ALBERT: We got a great task ahead of us, kid.

KARL: Exactly, we're writing history.

ALBERT: In blood, so be it. Like the Spartans. You don't know this 'cause you've been stuffed away in some girl's arsehole, but you can't become a man up your mother's dress, it will just never happen. Am I right?

Silence. KARL moves away to listen.

Old soldiers never die, they just keep talking on. Who said that?

KARL: Shh.

Silence.

ALBERT: Come on, that's an easy one. Old soldiers.

KARL: Don't know, shh.

ALBERT: Shame on you.

Silence.

HERRET: Richtofen.

ALBERT: Top of the class, little bureaucrat. The Baron. The Red Baron.

Silence.

KARL: Did he say anything about young soldiers?
ALBERT: [*well-informed*] Nothing.

Silence.

HERRET: They said—
ALBERT: Shut up.

Silence. KARL *comes back to* ALBERT *suddenly.*

KARL: Know what we are now? Werewolves. Those were the orders. Remember? If the district falls, you are to melt into Operation Werewolf. Sabotage. Stealth killing by yourself. Petrol bombs. Remember?

Silence.

HERRET: Not real werewolves, then.

ALBERT *looks at* HERRET, *is about to reprimand him—*

Distant speaker announcements in Russian.

Beat.

They move into action.

KARL: Up you go.

HERRET *scrambles reluctantly over* ALBERT *and the other two shove him up the ladder. He clings to the rungs, until we can only see his feet in the gloom.*

After a while HERRET *clambers down and squeezes past* ALBERT.

ALBERT: So? What do the Bolshevik Jew pig-monkeys say now?
HERRET: [*tending the lamp*] Sweep. Sweep the street once more, then report somewhere.
KARL: Somewhere?
HERRET: I don't know the word. Maybe mess tent? Soup tent, something?
KARL: Soup tent?
ALBERT: Are you deaf?
KARL: Yes, in this ear, completely, from whatever happened in the park.
ALBERT: Grenade.
KARL: Well, I don't remember.
ALBERT: Soup. Uh, soup.

All three groan involuntarily.

If anybody says how hungry they are I'll be forced to eat them.

HERRET: There's a whole black ham under our house, in— My uncle put it there and told me, promise, sir. Maybe we should sneak out while they're eating. Sir?

Silence.

I'll go. I can crawl along under the hedge and I won't move unless there's no-one and it's dark.

ALBERT: Why ask him?

KARL: My nose tells me everyone's dead, Pimpfy.

HERRET: Don't. You. Dare: They're civilians.

ALBERT: The gutter is filled with civilians, didn't you see? Mrs Threscher from the bakery, dead. All over the road, with fuckin' pink mush-tracks through their heads where the tanks have gone straight through 'em.

KARL: Just the bodies. Kid. Their spirits, are different. They get infused into the Reich. As long as they died fighting for the Führer.

ALBERT: Or they're swinging. Then they don't go nowhere.

Silence.

I saw two boys from school up the courtyard flagpole with Fidget. The brothers with the teeth. Whoever they were. But their heads were twice as big. The whole family was hiding. Fidget said. Hey there, Fidget, too slow.

Silence.

All the women are being raped I imagine now, or pressed on hot coals and eaten. That's what the capsules were for.

KARL: What capsules?

> HERRET *lashes out at* ALBERT. KARL *separates them quickly.* HERRET *refuses to cry.*

ALBERT: You little arsehole, what was that?

KARL: Shh. [*Beat.*] What capsules?

ALBERT: [*pointing at his Iron Cross*] I fucking kill people. I done it, I'll do it. I'll drown you. Want me to?

KARL: [*to* ALBERT] Answer the question, soldier.

Pause.

ALBERT: We had to hand them out. Those ones. While you were off playing with the big boys. They're for bureaucrats and bitches, babies. Cyanide, haven't you heard about them, blood… S'quick. Same as a… same as a bullet, I guess. Do that again, I'll kill you. On the spot.

Silence.

ALBERT *laughs hysterically for a while, then his sanity returns quickly.* KARL *joins in for at bit, at* HERRET*'s sulky expense.*

KARL: Fight bravely, die laughing.

ALBERT: I better not die, I haven't fucked yet.

KARL: It's not that good.

ALBERT: You never. You never ever.

Silence.

Who? Not that you did.

KARL: Shh.

Silence.

Margarate Tremayne. At the last dance.

ALBERT: You *never*— We're not even/ allowed to go.

KARL: Fidget and I, are you listening? Fidget and I, hid out behind that kitchen wall. Waited for five of them to come outside. We arranged. And yeah, we did, well I did, near the barrack fence.

ALBERT: Not the whole way you went I bet, no way.

Silence.

KARL: It was brilliant.

Silence.

ALBERT: Liar. Liar and a cheat.

KARL *punches* ALBERT*'s arm. Moves away to listen.*

That doesn't even hurt anymore.

KARL: Don't use that word, that's still a rule, that's forever. Don't you ever fucking call me that or I'll slice you down, son, I'll do it.

ALBERT: With what?

KARL: With my fingernails,/ teeth. Got it?

HERRET: Shh.

    Silence. KARL *touches his wound.*

ALBERT: Hey, did you see Hermes on the halftrack, were you there for that? Good soldier. That was... he did well, didn't he? You'd have to admit that. Fidget, down, would you say he went down well, 'cause I saw that, and Klober. See that? Yeah, you did. [*To* HERRET] See, Klober stands behind Willi's Panzerfaust, the one thing you don't do, kid. Willi, though, didn't he, hit the tank square on its damn flank— blang—it was a great shot, target-rich enriverment, enniver—

KARL: Environment.

ALBERT: It was a target-rich...

KARL: Environment.

ALBERT: Lotta tanks, and I turn around to run, and Klober... don't have a face no more./ He's just standing there sure, but no eyes, teeth, no nose, nothing. Lazy, grand scheme of things, huh? So he bought it. Saw that.

KARL: Albert.... Albert.

ALBERT: And good old oven-door Scholl who's now on my collar.

KARL: Wurtz... The day before the final examinations.

ALBERT: Cheat.

KARL: Scholl.

ALBERT: Dirty dog cheat.

KARL: I didn't cheat.

HERRET: Nobody cheated—/ shh.

KARL: Listen. Because all that's over: Scholl called me in after lights out, and told me that I'd won all the competitions months ago, that the tests were, and this is what he said, he says: It's all just... formality. He said. That you were always the weaker fellow—

ALBERT: Shame. Shame./ You lie.

HERRET: No no, quiet—

KARL: Hold your tongue, both of you. That I had to go wake you up and tell you you were weak, so I did, or else: I'd be demoted. I had to tell you so you'd think that's what I thought, and that you'd have to compete anyway, and then you'd go harder, so, just to make you, so you'd go harder, okay? You know I know you're not.

ALBERT: I'm not./ You did think that.

KARL: / Shut up. I didn't. No way.

Silence.

ALBERT: But you did.

KARL: Why would he do that?

ALBERT: Exactly. No reason. You just wanted to throw me off like a/ baby.

KARL: Wurtz. Why do you think he made me do that?

Silence.

ALBERT: No-one makes you do anything.

HERRET: Mutti does.

KARL *and* KARL *laugh, a single snort.*

ALBERT: Doesn't matter. I mean, I was promoted two weeks after, anyway, so. Then again, and again.

KARL: As was I. So.

Silence.

ALBERT: And you cheated in Capture the Flag the whole time.

KARL: I'm sorry to say I flogged your backside in Capture the Flag.

HERRET *giggles.*

ALBERT: I was robbed! At the bridge, you bureaucrat— You know I was bent over—/ arsehole!

HERRET: / Shhhh.

ALBERT: You're just saying that 'cause he's here.

KARL: Maybe you were's what I'm saying. They promoted us side by side from day one.

HERRET: You're not weaker.

KARL: Right? And we're slipped a mickey on the finish line: Me all along. Ask why? Why all you like. But they did. On my honour. [*He looks up.*] Damn, it's so long ago anyway.

ALBERT: Four months. Notice how you're too weak, to even, you know, reprimand me for swearing. You made crucial mistakes, everybody said, many times. In Capture the Flag, many times.

Silence.

KARL: That's nonsense. When?

The manhole is pulled open high above them. They push themselves into shadow and freeze. A weak beam of light makes it to the pipe.

ALBERT: Grenades. Karl, grenades.

KARL *shakes his head, listening. Finger to his lips.*

A bucket on a rope is lowered rapidly, almost hitting ALBERT. *It bobs in front of them.*

Silence.

There's food in it. Bread. Bacon. Smell it.

HERRET: Don't, it's a trap.

KARL: Good God, men, shut up.

Silence.

ALBERT: What if it's from someone on our side?

HERRET: What if it's over?

ALBERT: It's only food, I can see, there's a loaf under a rock. Why? I can take it and we'll run, Karl. Karl?

Silence.

From left: Sam North as Herret, Robin Goldsworthy as Albert and Anthony Gee as Karl in the 2007 Tamarama Rock Surfers production at the Old Fitzroy Theatre in Sydney. (Photo: Cam Baird)

KARL: Don't move, shut up.

> *A Russian voice calls down once: 'Don't starve to death, boys!'*
> *Silence.*

HERRET: He says don't starve, boys.

> *Silence.*

> ALBERT *moves towards the bucket, his face is right near it.*

KARL: [*even*] If you take it they will know we are down here.

> *The bucket slowly ascends.* ALBERT *jerks back and all are frozen again.*
> *Silence.*

> *The manhole is heard scraping and thunking shut again.*

> HERRET *is terrified.* KARL *takes the lantern from him and peers down the tunnels.*
> *Eventually he gives it back to* HERRET *and sits down.*
> *Silence.*

ALBERT: Firstly. When you were supposed to take the bridge and you sent all your besties in first, yeah you got the flag, but no-one left to get it back to base, did you? Secondly, um, when it was Protect the General and you got fatso Klobo up the shitpipe by lying low, and the time you didn't take me in the rushes, the day at the lake, my win thanks, so: Disastrous choices.

> KARL *takes off his badges and throws them in the water.*

KARL: I relieve myself of rank. I dissolve the unit.

ALBERT: Then it goes to me.

KARL: Sure, though you'll officially command yourself. We're lone wolves, dress as civilians. It's all different now.

ALBERT: But you officially step down.

KARL: That's over.

> ALBERT *retrieves the badge.* KARL *manages to rip a few more insignias from his uniform.*

ALBERT: Don't get caught in uniform? Coward.

KARL: Who said anything about getting caught. Take the war back to the street, as individual units, was the order. This is what we're doing.

ALBERT: You've lost it, son. There has to be a leader.

KARL: Listen. Scholl got back from the Front, from Cobra, right? And he said. At some point. In fire fight. Every soldier becomes a one-man platoon.

HERRET: Can I go, then?

ALBERT: No. You're staying in rank right there, I'm in charge. Rule One: My body belongs to my nation. Say it.

HERRET: My body belongs to my nation.

ALBERT: Firstly. I beat you in Archery.

Silence.

Admit it.

KARL: Archery was the day my… my parents got dragged out of bed by their hair, Albert.

HERRET *puts his hands over his ears.*

The maid told me dragged. Found a curl of mother's hair near the gate and father's purse in the bedpan, he threw it there, for me to find, I believe.

ALBERT: We know.

HERRET: I'm being invisible now.

Silence.

ALBERT: They were scum though. I mean that's what you said.

KARL: [*with difficulty*] Don't speak.

ALBERT: No, that's what you said.

KARL: If you… Don't speak no more for a bit.

ALBERT: You can't make me.

KARL: Can and will.

Silence.

You think that all that was true? You met my… you met them, Albert. I said that, yes, because I had to say that in parade for Scholl and all to hear and see but did you see my eyes man, blood, I was, up there, screaming through my face: There was no joke. No BBC. I said: If you say he's scum, sir, then he is—that's all I was forced to admit, and, and—he's at the bank seven days a week for— Why would they? My God, he never told a joke in his life, I promise, Wurtz.

Silence.

We sent word anyway, they're probably fine, especially because he's innocent as day, I tell you, and my aunt got word to an officer that it was all a mistake, and he agreed, so. I'll thump you out of the Reich if you say scum again.

Silence.

ALBERT: You won't hit your superior.
KARL: What?
ALBERT: [*louder*] You won't hit your superior.
KARL: We'll see. It's not Archery anymore.
ALBERT: Your orders are shut your hole. Look. If they listened to the BBC Imperialists, then they did, if they weren't, like you said, exactly, as you said, hell man, pull in your lip.
KARL: No hard feelings was the point, Al. End of the day it's just a fucking badge.
ALBERT: It's a symbol.
KARL: Werewolves.
HERRET: Shh.
ALBERT: Wire up.
HERRET: Quiet!

Silence. They listen.

KARL: Did you fart, Albert?

They giggle.

A noise down the pipe. They recoil and freeze.

Silence.

ALBERT: Just rats, kid.

We hear rats. Silence.

They have to move again to keep warm.
I could eat five rats. [*He laughs bitterly.*] I can taste it.

Silence.

Off you go then, werewolf.

KARL: We're all werewolves. Waiting for our moment to surface. Split up. Strike.

Silence.

At least we don't have to listen to Scholly screaming at us anymore.

ALBERT: At least we don't have to listen to you yelling at us anymore.

KARL: At least we got that T-34. Nailed it. Smoke pouring out of it.

HEERET: At least all the animals from the zoo can go and live in the woods now. They bombed the zoo, they all got out.

ALBERT: We know.

Silence.

KARL: Brr.

KARL *sings quite softly.* ALBERT *joins in.*

KARL & ALBERT: [*sung*]

> Ever faithful shall I be
> Even if I'm left alone,
> I might be mad and laughing
> But forward I'll be marching.
> This flag isn't falling till I do.
>
> It shall cover my corpse like a shroud,
> It shall cover my corpse like a shroud.

KARL: Heil/ Hitler.

ALBERT: Heil Hitler.

Silence. They look at HERRET *who stares at the lamp.*

I say we go that way, right now. Back there is the way we had to get in, up is now, in my opinion a fucked option, leaving… that way.

Silence.

You'd never guess.

Silence.

You know how my mother went to stay with my grandparents in Flasburg?

Silence.

Well. I—ha—idiots.

Silence.

I heard her talking about evacuating, right? Weeks ago. Heard her loudly, proudly, talking, in the kitchen, my mum and my sister, for the whole block to hear. So I told her when I walked in I heard everything. You've got one hour, if they wanted to disgrace me and go running, she's got one hour before I go tell Scholl; that's how she tested me, so that's what she got. Deserting. She packed just one bag, in a few minutes she was gone with my sister. The house is mine now. I'm going to rebuild it, after this is, ah… finished.

> *Silence.*

KARL: That was a hard thing you did.

ALBERT: Hard as Krupp steel, old man.

KARL: [*shivering*] It's best they left, as women, yes?

ALBERT: That or the capsules. Or the coals.

KARL: We done good so far, that's for sure.

> *Silence.*

ALBERT: I don't suppose we'll ever play Capture the Flag again.

> HERRET *produces a capsule.*

HERRET: I have a capsule.

> ALBERT *takes it off him.*

Hey!

ALBERT: / You're not messing around with that, that's for babies and milk cows, you're a soldier now, understand?

KARL: Let me see it.

ALBERT: Go order yourself around, why don't you?

> ALBERT *pockets the capsule.*

HERRET: I'm supposed to trade that for food—

> *There is the sound of a something landing in water, then…*

KARL: Shit.

> *A grenade explosion somewhere in the drain system. Then an aftershock.*

> *The reverberations are a sudden, severe force. (A few seconds slow motion under special lights was effective in the original*

production.) The boys are thrown in the water, and there they stay frozen for a long time.

Silence. Darkness—rather blues.

KARL *can't stand the cold any longer. With a gasp he sits up and looks around frantically for the enemy. The others do the same.*

ALBERT: [*panting*] Damn. Oh, oh. Damn it.

HERRET: / Shh.

KARL: Wait—

ALBERT: Blood that's cold.

They pant and shudder and moan. They shake themselves, trying to locate warmth. ALBERT *strips his sodden coat. They huddle together, one mass pulled into form by* KARL.

KARL: Wait just a bit longer—

ALBERT: We can't go up now.

KARL: That's what—I know.

ALBERT: We should have gone before. Oh hell, my feet.

KARL: Shh.

ALBERT: My feet's gone.

ALBERT *and* HERRET *keep an eye on the end of the drain where the sound came from. They regain control of their breath.*

Silence as they settle, drip, shiver. KARL *is in trouble, he is freezing to death.*

At some point HERRET *manages to relight the lamp with matches kept safe.*

Did you really? With Margarate Tremayne?

KARL: Ha.

ALBERT: Did you rape her, did you?

KARL: Don't be stupid. You don't know anything.

Silence.

It was so good. The kissing part was soft, like everyone says, and good. And the band was playing and everything.

Silence.

ALBERT: I bet it was fantastic. Tell me.

KARL: The grass was wet. But it was warm back then. The moon. Trucks going past on the other side of the fence. She didn't take much off-f. L-like I said. The sex bit was pretty stupid.

ALBERT: I am fucking every woman after the war, every one. I wouldn't think sex with Margarate Tremayne's that stupid. You're stupid. Nuts. I would get the badge for Fucking Margarate Tremayne Properly I bet.

KARL: We were still winning at the dance.

ALBERT: Properly. While you do night reconnaissance in your bloody socks, with cut feet. Hey. Comrade? [*He separates himself.*] Why did you every day, every single day, dish out punishment so hard?

HERRET *tries to move away.*

HERRET: [*looking down the pipe suddenly*] Mama?

KARL: Shh. Don't be retarded, there's no-one there.

ALBERT: You never had to punch me so hard./ Bastard.

KARL: I did have to—shh. Keep warm.

ALBERT: Twice you smiled, even—admit it. Admit it, admit it.

ALBERT *is hissing.*

KARL: When?

HERRET: Don't punch, look at the lamp./ Sir?

ALBERT: / Liar— Every day?

Silence.

Every day?

He lashes out at KARL *who lets him for a while then shoves him off hard.* ALBERT *falls over* HERRET *who is protecting the lamp.*

ALBERT *lies in the water.*

Silence.

HERRET: Get up. You'll freeze.

ALBERT *chuckles.*

ALBERT: I would lose. Both my eyes. To kiss Margarate Tremayne. Just once.

Silence.

What lovely girls there are in the world.

KARL pulls ALBERT out of the water, the effort nearly cripples him. KARL inspects his wound.

Okay—

KARL: I am no longer in a position… to…

ALBERT: Okay. Everyone promise. No punching for rat-holing. Deal?… Deal.

He produces a square of chocolate. He divides it. They all take a piece.

Shh. Just be—shh.

KARL just holds his piece. ALBERT eats his automatically. HERRET, torn between keeping it and eating it, eats it.

I think I might have, um, shot Fidget in the hip. He was running away, so. He was already falling…

KARL: So.

ALBERT: So. I'm pretty sure I shot him above his belt. Will I swing for that?

KARL: No.

ALBERT: He was in the way… Lazy is what he was—so… I really would say that.

KARL: It's different now. L-listen.

ALBERT: You gonna eat that? Hey. Did you hear this? When you were away, they gave Fatso Klober a platoon for a day, and he lost the flag every battle, over and over, so at lunch his platoon gets none, right? They're starving. Next battle after lunch, we find his HQ, kill the guards, and my guys come into where he's hiding and Klober's got the flag in his mouth, and he's trying to eat it.

KARL: [*tiny*] Yeah.

ALBERT: He was, eating the flag. 'You can't capture it if it's in me!'—all crying. He was crying, all blubbing. Blubbery. Too slow anyway, Klobo, sack of bum-flaps.

There is a sound down the end of the drain they came from. They are very still.

Here we go.

KARL: [*clear*] Knife.

ALBERT *draws his and thinks about giving it to* KARL *but doesn't.*

HERRET *desperately draws his blunt dagger and gives it to* KARL, *then gets behind them.*

They press their backs flat against the pipe. KARL *stoops and hesitates before killing the lamp.*

Wait for the last Ivan to pass. Saw the larynx. One move. Foot in the back.

ALBERT: Foot in the back.

HERRET: They're too big.

KARL: Disarm.

ALBERT: Kill the fucking light.

The lamp is cloaked. The sound sloshes nearer.

A light appears. A torch wavers, slowly approaching. It stops and the beam turns on the three boys' faces, frozen.

MATHILDE, *fifteen, shines the torch in her own face.*

MATHILDE: It's just me. You're all as scared as me.

The light searches into the gloom again, returning to MATHILDE'*s face.*

Is there anyone else down here?

Silence.

Any soldiers?

She shines the torch in their faces again as ALBERT *lights a match and relights the lamp, dimmer now.* MATHILDE *is a civilian in relatively clean clothes.*

Of course not.

Silence. MATHILDE *sits with them.*

KARL: What's happened?

MATHILDE: They came in and tied my mother to the table so I ran. From the cupboard. Just then. They let me run, maybe chased me, maybe, maybe didn't see me but I ran very, ah, very hard. They haven't touched me. But, hey ho, what do you know. I'm, ah, preparing for it, right now, I'm, so very alert I can't stop my heart. Are they down here?

Silence.

KARL: Werewolves?

MATHILDE: What? No, all that's over.

KARL: That's. What werewolves make you think.

She inspects their faces with the torch.

MATHILDE: It's finished, boys.

ALBERT: We're not boys, I'm Jungzugfuhrer Wurtz, Heil Hitler. Operation Werewolf's a real thing.

HERRET *hugs* MATHILDE.

He's useless.

KARL: That's it?

MATHILDE: Have you any food down here?

ALBERT: Shh.

KARL: That's it?

ALBERT: Answer him.

MATHILDE: No? Just orders, huh? Well, yesterday three officers just stood in the street and… put their guns in their mouths.

MATHILDE *pries* HERRET *off her, and moves to look down the pipe.*

KARL: Ivan?

MATHILDE: Ivan is everywhere.

HERRET: It's all over now, Jungzugfuhrer. Isn't it?

ALBERT: Shut up.

MATHILDE: For you, maybe. Surrender. You'll be treated like civilians if you take off your badges. Take off your badges.

KARL: No surrender.

ALBERT: Hear that, Pimpfy? Precisely. It's just different rules now. Werewolf rules now.

Silence as MATHILDE *sits between them. She keeps her torch on for comfort, tucked in her crossed arms. It casts a ghoulish up-light.*

ALBERT *toys with taking his badges off but doesn't.*

MATHILDE: What have all the men gone and done? How old are you?

ALBERT: Fuck off. It doesn't matter, we're the last bullet. Our honour is loyalty. When the Fatherland needs you, do you step aside, no, up, eyes front, smile till the end.

MATHILDE *points her torch.*

MATHILDE: How old are you?
HERRET: Eight.

   Silence.

ALBERT: We're both twelve.
KARL: I think we did okay.

   Silence.

ALBERT: They may be everywhere now. We'll find our moment—shh.
MATHILDE: To what?
ALBERT: Shh. To strike.
MATHILDE: No. For me to run. For you to surrender.
ALBERT: Ha! Shame. We can fight for fifty years, he said.
KARL: What if. We done our jobs now, Wurtz.
ALBERT: Your body belongs to your nation.
KARL: I know, R-rule One.

   Silence.

From left: Sam North as Herret, Ella Scott Lynch as Mathilde, Robin Goldsworthy as Albert and Anthony Gee as Karl in the 2007 Tamarama Rock Surfers production at the Old Fitzroy Theatre in Sydney.
(Photo: Cam Baird)

I never got the other nine. Number one, sure. It's yours. Take it. Who cares about the other nine?

ALBERT: Coward.

KARL: [*smiling*] Not me. Youmustbelookinattamirror. [*The last words come as he's cramping.*] I'm as firm as the most German of trees, the mighty oak.../ So.

ALBERT: Some things are over, sure, yes, we have to do it different like you said, but—it's just different, it's not over. We spill our blood, right? We do what we're fucking trained for, pity's sake—Heil Hitler. I'm—we're trained, so we do it, one hundred percent. Simple. You're not stopping me from dying.

KARL: As if I would.

ALBERT: I'm getting my Knight's Cross, son.

KARL: How could I?

ALBERT: I'm getting my fuckin' swords and fucking leaves.

> MATHILDE *protests.*

KARL: It's how you die, remember? Like all those swingers.

ALBERT: I know.

KARL: They die mean and stupid. Everyone dies.

MATHILDE: No, listen, they're being kind to you, boys,/ surrender.

KARL: I beg your pardon, Fräulein, but we die.

> *Silence.*

And what if my mother and father are dead, what if? Then they died honest, trust me. Remember? It just has to be honest, not mean. And so far we done real good. So when we're soaked back into the trees, and the rocks, the lakes, we'll all see each other again.

ALBERT: I say we go that way right now.

> *Silence.*

Or just let me think for a minute.

MATHILDE: Yes, keep thinking, that's all we have to do. Keep thinking, keep thinking, keep thinking...

ALBERT: Shut up.

MATHILDE: Think about, what, I don't know, anything, keep thinking anything for warmth, boys. Do it. Anything. Cowboys. Jungles.

HERRET: They're right above us.

MATHILDE: I know.

Silence.

ALBERT *watches* KARL *for a while.*

There was a concert. Were you boys there for that? Last week, I can't, I mean it was a wonderful concert—oh, it was marvellous, it was the very definition of what marvellous is—it soared, that's what you always read, that 'it soars', but it soared, and it made me marvel. You have to believe me. Waves of music, boys, washing through the house, reaching into everyone with whooshing wings, you could feel it on your face even where we were, my mother and I were standing right at the top up the back. Half the audience could only stand. He was there (I only saw half his face) …

KARL: Mama.

MATHILDE: … Oh, it was just movement after movement, they kept… going, they played on far far past the finishing time, and then it just stopped, and you couldn't hear a thing, everyone was holding their breath—everyone at once, imagine it—and the conductor turned and he coughs and then he tells us it's over. And only then does everyone start applauding, everyone stood up at once, jump to our feet and it was the loudest clapping I've ever heard, really, this cracking, cracking, on and on, no-one wanted to stop. They had to break it up, send us out. Then on the steps… you boys, rows and rows, one on each step. With boxes. With your boxes of capsules. Mother told me off for reaching for one, only because others were doing as much— Was it one of you little things? Who I nearly took one from? I asked her what they were for, she said nothing. Nothing. She could have told me, I think. Do any of you have capsules?

HERRET *looks at* ALBERT.

ALBERT: Karl. If it is over. Like you said. And everything is different. Rules are new, and what's happened has happened, then it doesn't change the flag in the grand scheme, because, as you said. We did what was asked, we did what they said, what you said, whenever it was said—jump, how bloody high, right? Never failed, never weakened. If it's over then. If.

Silence.

Know that when you called me a weakling, which you meant when you said it—bastard. When I got robbed like that. That, that set certain things. To this. But if it's over then.

Silence.

'Cause I rang the number. On the downstairs telephone during a raid. The number that they say you have to ring if you hear anything, you know, the bloody law at the end of the film—yeah, you know the film—damn, at least we don't have to watch those damn films anymore, if it's over. I did that, and told them that your parents had made the joke about Stalingrad. And that maybe, only maybe, they had heard it on the Imperial gangster BBC. Because Fidget said that and who else would have told you something like that, right, I mean come on, that, and everyone had heard you say it, blood, you admitted it, so you know, that was that, that they did: that's that, but if everything's different then I should say that—you should know that, that's fair, if you called me a weakling even though I never cried when you beat me and you still get all the glory ahead of me—that's fine—'cause I get to say that. That I did that. There. You know. Heil Hitler.

Silence.

Karl? Are you listening?

KARL *is dead.* ALBERT *touches him and he falls in the water.*

MATHILDE: Are they going to come down here do you think? Boys? Look at me.
HERRET: He said we were in a hedgehog. He said no-one could get in.
ALBERT: Karl.

Silence.

MATHILDE: A prayer. That's what we need. Fend off the cold. Someone say one. Don't look at him.

Silence.

ALBERT: I only know… the—
MATHILDE: Not that one. A different one.

HERRET *keeps his eyes open and stares at the lamp.*

HERRET: Dear God... I'm sorry if I'm interrupting. I only asked once, and I know it was more begging.

ALBERT: Pray for bullets, why don't you?/ Ha.

HERRET: It was only once before, if you remember, and you listened then, and I've thanked you so many times since then for that, but thank you again, and I've been strong at not calling on you—

ALBERT *laughs, once, lost, cries a bit.*

With things being tough, since, um... Yes, praying's meant to be secret too and only in my skull, but things have got pretty bad. So. There's, um, please help us find the people we care for dearly, for they must be worried about us. Even if, for all of us, there might be only one person left, please help us find that person or help them find us. So—

ALBERT: What happened to the miracle weapon, you think?

Silence.

HERRET: I know—

ALBERT: Huh?

Silence.

HERRET: I—

ALBERT: That might still happen.

Silence.

HERRET: So. I know you're very busy right now, but as I said before, I haven't asked for anything since Mutti fell ill, and if everything's finished now...We're very hungry too, God. We do need food, sorry to say. Please don't let us end up... like the, ah, boy we found in the cellar. If you can help us we will not be scared at all, we promise. And please if you can try to make sure Mutti is not in pain. Thank you, God. Amen.

MATHILDE: Amen.

ALBERT: Heil Hitler.

MATHILDE: Where's he now, do you think?

ALBERT *bites the capsule and dies. Foam comes out of his mouth, he wheezes, then leans back and stays there.*

Silence.

That foam. Is all over the city now.

Silence. HERRET *and the* MATHILDE *draw nearer.*

Don't be scared.

Silence.

HERRET: I'm not.

MATHILDE: I'm sorry to ask, but. When they take me, what shall I do, do you think?

HERRET: Try to look old. That's what my Mutti said.

> MATHILDE *tries, but can't, she is simply too young.* HERRET *laughs. She laughs, then tries not to cry.*

MATHILDE: I'm not much of an actor. They took the girl who lives below us yesterday. She was hiding under her bed. And when they got to the stairs, she started screaming my name. Saying: 'Take her. Take her. She's up there.' So we waited and waited. But they didn't come. Until today. I always said good morning to her.

HERRET: I can't stay here.

MATHILDE: I have this feeling… You know how he always said we will be remembered, these days. I can't help feel, no it won't. I mean, armies, got here, will be remembered, yes of course, that's obvious. But this? My mother just now, on the table with them hitting her—*she's still up there.* They're hitting her in the face. And boot-polish all over the walls, all the paintings are all knocked off, fallen down.

> *Silence.*

I mean, who will know that? I feel that that no-one will. Huh. Maybe it shouldn't be known. That's probably it. Ha. Well. Warm yourself on this, little one. It can't get any colder.

> *There is a noise above. Then silence. They both look up, frozen.*
>
> *The noise of a distant manhole being scraped open above. A very weak beam of cold daylight enshrouds the two of them. Faint Russian voices drift down. Then a shout.*
>
> MATHILDE *jerks back. They are frozen for a moment.*
>
> *Music: Ludvig van Beethoven—Piano Trio in D Major, Op. 70 No. 1 'Ghost' (2nd movement).*
>
> HERRET *starts rapidly pulling out fistfuls of capsules from his pockets.*

HERRET: I don't want them.

He pulls out more, dropping them in her lap. More and more. The last of them rain down on her.

HERRET *moves* ALBERT *aside.*

HERRET *is about to climb up the ladder when he hesitates.*

He turns back and kisses MATHILDE. *Then he clambers up the ladder towards the light, eventually disappearing.* MATHILDE *watches him go.*

MATHILDE *looks at the capsules in her lap. She looks down the pipe, peering into the darkness, in the direction nobody has come from yet. At the bodies. Smoothes her hair, and puts a capsule in her mouth. The music rises.*

She spits it out then sweeps the capsules off her. Turns on her torch. And stands.

She moves into the darkness, disappearing. Her torchlight disappears.

The weak beam of light from outside becomes brighter as the tunnel fades, then blinks to darkness suddenly.

Sound of a manhole closing above.

* * *

Other titles suitable for teenage audiences

ENGINE
By Janis Balodis

Set in the aftermath of the death of a young boy in a car accident, *Engine* is a funny and moving roller-coaster story of young people and cars, about fixing what's broken and celebrating life.

978-0-86819-889-7   PB

BOY OVERBOARD (the play)
Adapted by Patricia Cornelius

Adapted from Morris Gleitzman's best-selling novel, *Boy Overboard* depicts a deeply human side of the 'asylum seekers' issue by following the journey of a brother and sister from Afghanistan to Australia. Based on real life events, this is a moving play about young people overcoming the confusion of war, politics and the search for a safe haven.

978-0-86819-807-1   PB

THURSDAY'S CHILD (the play)
Adapted by Eva di Cesare /Sandra Eldridge /Tim McGarry

Sonya Hartnett's surreal and epic story of an Australian farming family's strength as they battle their way through the great depression of the 1930s has been beautifully adapted to the stage by Monkey Baa.

978-0-86819-887-3   PB

HITLER'S DAUGHTER (the play)
Adapted by Eva di Cesare /Sandra Eldridge /Tim McGarry

Four country children waiting in the rain for the school bus take turns telling stories. In an unusual twist, Anna's story takes the children to Nazi Germany. This intriguing play—adapted from Jackie French's novel—poses powerful questions about a frightening period in history and forces us to examine moral issues in relation to society's fears and prejudices in a fresh, compelling light.

978-0-86819-813-2   PB

ZEAL THEATRE COLLECTION

By Stefo Nantsou and Tom Lycos

The Stones is based on a true story of two boys charged with manslaughter after throwing rocks from a freeway overpass and killing a motorist. *Taboo*, commissioned by the Sydney Theatre Company, deals with date rape, internet dating, and the ripple effects of sexual assault. *Burnt* was born out of the true stories of people from regional Australia struggling with prolonged drought, and how the stresses and strains of continued drought impacts on families and young people.

978-0-86819-906-1   PB

STORIES IN THE DARK

By Debra Oswald

When Tomas, a 12-year-old trapped in a war-torn city, finds himself separated from his family he takes refuge in a derelict house with 16-year-old Anna. Anna tells Tomas folk stories to distract them both from the horrors outside. *Stories in the Dark* explores the power of storytelling, mingling the magic and earthy wisdom of folk tales with the hard-edged story of violence, conflict and the struggle to survive.

978-0-86819-831-6   PB

THE BOOK OF EVERYTHING (the play)

Adapted by Richard Tulloch

Thomas is nine and he's started writing a book. His father says all important books are about God. Even so, Thomas writes down all the interesting things he sees that other people seem to ignore: tropical fish in the canal, a deluge of frogs, the Son of God popping in for a chat … He also writes down his greatest determination: When I grow up, I'm going to be happy.A totally magical story about a child learning to act when faced with fear and wrong-doing.

978-0-86819-933-7   PB

www.currency.com.au

Visit Currency Press' website now to:

- Buy your books online
- Browse through our full list of titles, from plays to screenplays, books on theatre, film and music, and more
- Choose a play for your school or amateur performance group by cast size and gender
- Obtain information about performance rights
- Find out about theatre productions and other performing arts news across Australia
- For students, read our study guides
- For teachers, access syllabus and other relevant information
- Sign up for our email newsletter

The performing arts publisher

www.ingramcontent.com/pod-product-compliance
Lightning Source LLC
Chambersburg PA
CBHW041935090426
42744CB00017B/2067